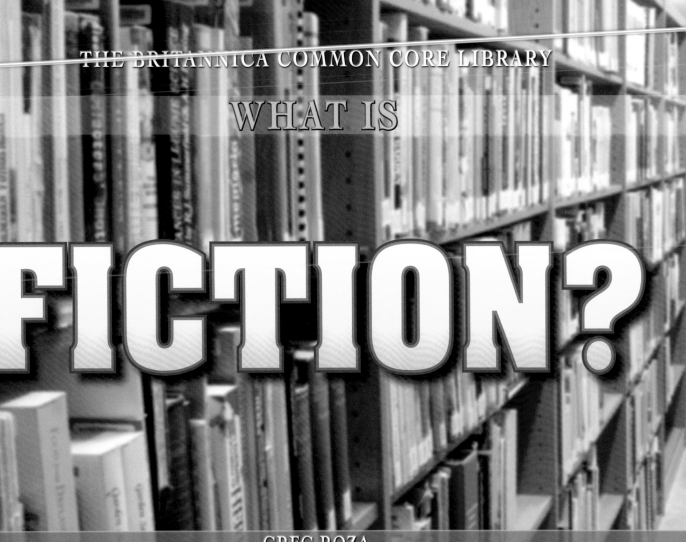

THE BRITANNICA COMMON CORE LIBRARY

WHAT IS

FICTION?

GREG ROZA

Britannica®
Educational Publishing

IN ASSOCIATION WITH

ROSEN
EDUCATIONAL SERVICES

Published in 2015 by Britannica Educational Publishing (a trademark of Encyclopædia Britannica, Inc.) in association with The Rosen Publishing Group, Inc.
29 East 21st Street, New York, NY 10010

Distributed exclusively by Rosen Publishing.
To see additional Britannica Educational Publishing titles, go to rosenpublishing.com.

First Edition

Britannica Educational Publishing
J. E. Luebering: Director, Core Reference Group
Mary Rose McCudden: Editor, Britannica Student Encyclopedia

Rosen Publishing
Hope Lourie Killcoyne: Executive Editor
Heather Moore Niver: Editor
Nelson Sá: Art Director
Nicole Russo: Designer
Cindy Reiman: Photography Manager
Karen Huang: Photo Researcher

Library of Congress Cataloging-in-Publication Data

Roza, Greg.
What is Fiction?/Greg Roza. — First Edition.
      pages cm. — (The Britannica Common Core Library)
Includes bibliographical references and index.
ISBN 978-1-62275-660-5 (library bound) — ISBN 978-1-62275-661-2 (pbk.) — ISBN 978-1-62275-662-9 (6-pack)
1. Fiction — History and criticism — Juvenile literature. 2. Fiction — Authorship — Juvenile literature. 3. Books and reading — Juvenile literature. I. Title.
PN3491.R69 2015
809.3 — dc23
                                                                                          20140153

Manufactured in the United States of America

CONTENTS

What Is Fiction?

Writers use their imagination to create a kind of **literature** called fiction. They invent characters, put them in a setting, and give them feelings, words, and adventures.

Fiction is written in a style called **prose**, which is much like everyday speech. The other main type of prose is nonfiction, which is based on facts and true stories.

Many people enjoy reading fiction.

Literature is writing that is usually considered to be a work of art.

Prose is the ordinary language used in speaking or writing.

You can find many works of fiction at your school or neighborhood library.

Modern fiction comes in two main forms: the novel and the short story. A novel can tell a long and complicated story. It can have many parts—called chapters—and many characters. A short novel is sometimes called a novella.

Short stories are shorter than novels. They usually have fewer characters and only a few important scenes.

Where Did Fiction Come From?

Today, stories are still an important part of our culture, just as they were thousands of years ago.

Thousands of years ago people expressed ideas about the world by telling stories aloud. They usually told stories as poetry to make them easier to remember. Eventually people began writing them down so they could not be changed or lost.

Over time story forms changed and fiction was written. Cultures all over the world developed their own collections of short stories and novels.

Fiction Writers

Don Quixote is often called the first modern novel. The Spanish writer Miguel de Cervantes completed it in 1615.

In the Middle East and Asia storytellers told the tales of the *Arabian Nights*, or *The Thousand and One Nights*. These short stories were collected and written down in the 800s or 900s.

In the 1000s the Japanese writer Murasaki Shikibu wrote *The Tale of Genji*. Many consider this story of a Japanese prince to be the world's oldest novel.

This picture shows a scene from "Aladdin," which is one of the stories in Arabian Nights.

Elements of Fiction

There are many kinds of fiction. Some common types of fiction include science fiction, romance, mystery, fantasy, thriller, realistic fiction, and humor.

All works of fiction are made up of parts called literary elements. The most common literary elements include plot (or story), setting (or place), character, point of view, theme (or main subject), and conflict (or struggle).

Adventure stories are filled with action, suspense, and memorable characters.

Fiction Writers

In Judy Blume's humorous novel *Superfudge*, the central conflict is between the main character, Peter, and his troublesome little brother, Fudge. The story is told from Peter's point of view.

Each piece of fiction uses these literary elements differently. For example, the conflict in a story could be between two characters, it could be between a character and a force of nature, or it could be a struggle a character has within himself or herself. How a story is told also differs greatly among works. Some stories are told from the point of view of a character within the story. Others are told by someone outside of the story.

Judy Blume has written 28 books, including three for adult readers. Her work has been translated into 32 languages.

Passages from Great Fiction

The following examples show how six great works of fiction use literary elements differently.

A Horse's Point of View

Anna Sewell wrote *Black Beauty* in 1877. The novel is told from the point of view of the main character, a horse.

> There were six young colts in the meadow besides me; they were older than I was;

From this early passage in Sewell's novel, readers learn that Black Beauty *is a young colt who shares a meadow with other colts. What else do we learn from this passage?*

Fiction Writers

Sewell said she wrote *Black Beauty* to encourage people to treat horses with understanding and kindness.

some were nearly as large as grown-up horses. I used to run with them, and had great fun; we used to gallop all together round and round the field as hard as we could go. Sometimes we had rather rough play, for they would **frequently** bite and kick as well as gallop.

Frequently means often.

Black Beauty was Anna Sewell's only novel. It became the first major animal story in children's literature.

Like the setting described in this passage, Scrooge himself was a cheerless character who mistreated others.

A Cheerless Setting

A grumpy man named Ebenezer Scrooge is the main character in the ghost story *A Christmas Carol*. This passage describes Scrooge's surroundings at the beginning of the story.

> It was cold, **bleak**, biting weather ... and he could hear the people in the court outside, go wheezing up and down, beating their hands upon their breasts,

Fiction Writers

Charles Dickens published *A Christmas Carol* in 1843.

and stamping their feet upon the pavement stones to warm them. The city clocks had only just gone three, but it was quite dark already—it had not been light all day—and candles were flaring in the windows of the neighbouring offices … The fog came pouring in at every **chink** and keyhole, and was so dense without, that … the houses opposite were mere phantoms.

Charles Dickens also wrote Oliver Twist (1838), which tells the story of an orphan boy in London. In many of his later books, Dickens wrote about social problems that worried him.

Bleak means cheerless.

A **chink** is a narrow break in a wall.

Let's Compare

The passages have different settings and narrations.

> The way that a story is told is called **narration**.

Sewell's passage takes place in a meadow. Words like "great fun," "gallop," "round and round" and "rough" help the reader understand that the meadow is an active, enjoyable place for the horses that can sometimes be difficult. Dickens's passage describes a cold, foggy city street. Words like "biting," "wheezing," "beating," "dense," and "phantoms" help show how miserable the setting is both on the street and inside the offices.

The narration of Dickens's passage is in the third person, which means the teller uses "he" or "she" or "they" when talking about the characters in the story.

The passages by Sewell and Dickens create a tone, or mood. The tone of Sewell's passage is light and fun. What is the mood in Sewell's passage? How would you describe the tone of Dickens's passage? Reread the passages. Which words help you understand the tone of each passage.

Sewell's passage uses first-person narration. Black Beauty uses "I" to tell his own story.

Conflict Between Characters

This passage from *Anne of Green Gables* (1908) describes a conflict between the novel's redheaded main character, Anne, and a boy in her class named Gilbert.

Gilbert reached across the aisle, picked up the end of Anne's long red braid ... and said in a piercing whisper: "Carrots! Carrots!"

Then Anne looked at him with a **vengeance**!

She did more than look. She sprang to her feet, her bright fancies fallen into cureless ruin. She flashed one indignant glance at

Montgomery continued to write books about Anne Shirley, following the character from girlhood to adulthood.

Fiction Writers

Lucy Maud Montgomery used her childhood journal entries to write *Anne of Green Gables*.

Gilbert from eyes whose angry sparkle was swiftly **quenched** in equally angry tears.

"You mean, hateful boy!" she exclaimed passionately. "How dare you!"

And then—thwack! Anne had brought her **slate** down on Gilbert's head and cracked it— slate not head—clear across.

Vengeance is anger over an insult.

Quenched means put out.

Slate is a chalkboard tablet.

Many films, TV shows, and plays retell Montgomery's original novel. This image from a 1934 film version of the novel shows two actors acting out the words in this passage.

Many characters and story events in the 1939 film The Wizard of Oz *differ from those in Baum's novel.*

A Wicked Character

As her name suggests, the Wicked Witch of the West, from L. Frank Baum's *The Wonderful Wizard of Oz* (1900), is a mean character.

Now the Wicked Witch of the West had but one eye, yet that was as powerful as a telescope, and could see everywhere. So, as she sat in the door of her castle, she happened to look around and saw Dorothy lying asleep, with her friends all about her. They were a

Fiction Writers

Baum wrote a total of 14 books about Oz.

The Broadway musical Wicked *tells a different story about the Wicked Witch and her fellow witch, Glinda.*

long distance off, but the Wicked Witch was angry to find them in her country; so she blew upon a silver whistle that hung around her neck.

At once there came running to her from all directions a pack of great wolves. They had long legs and fierce eyes and sharp teeth.

"Go to those people," said the Witch, "and tear them to pieces."

Let's Compare

The main character in each of these passages has a conflict with another character that leads to an attack. But the **motives** for the attacks are very different.

Montgomery uses words like "indignant" and "angry sparkle" to show that Anne is very hurt when Gilbert calls her Carrots. It is clear that Anne's attack on Gilbert is an

The conflict between Anne and Gilbert may cause readers to ask a number of questions. Why did Gilbert call Anne "Carrots"? Why does Anne react so strongly to it? Will the two characters ever get along?

> A **motive** is a desire or need that causes a character to do something.
>
> A **villain** in a story is a character who is mean and does bad things.

instant reaction to his treatment of her. She wants to get back at him for hurting her feelings.

Baum does not help readers understand the Wicked Witch of the West's motive for wanting Dorothy and her friends torn to pieces. Instead, he makes it clear by the witch's name and by her actions that she is a **villain** of the worst sort. She wants to hurt Dorothy and her friends just because they are in her country.

Actress and singer Judy Garland played Dorothy in the 1939 movie The Wizard of Oz.

Subject of Survival

The Call of the Wild (1903), by Jack London, is about a dog named Buck who is stolen from his home and sold to work as a sled dog.

Buck's first day on the Dyea beach was like a nightmare. Every hour was filled with shock and surprise. He had been suddenly jerked from the heart of civilization and flung into the heart of things **primordial**...

Similar to Black Beauty, *the main character of* The Call of the Wild *is an animal that must deal with several different kinds of owners.*

Fiction Writers

Before writing Buck's story, London himself had traveled to Arctic areas similar to his novel's setting. In 1906, London wrote another novel called White Fang. It, too, uses the Arctic as part of its setting.

The Call of the Wild appeared in parts in the Saturday Evening Post *during the summer of 1903. Readers eagerly awaited the next installment of this classic adventure novel.*

Here was neither peace, nor rest, nor a moment's safety. All was confusion and action, and every moment life and limb were in peril. There was **imperative** need to be constantly alert; for these dogs and men were not town dogs and men. They were savages, all of them, who knew no law but the law of club and fang.

Primordial means basic.

Imperative means very important.

Plot of Suspense

Edgar Allan Poe published his short story "The Tell-Tale Heart" in 1843. In it, a madman tells how he kills an old man and hides the body beneath the floorboards. Later, the madman hears the beating of the old man's heart as he is questioned by police.

The ringing became more distinct ... I talked more freely to get rid of the feeling: but it continued and gained definiteness until, at length, I

Today, Poe is remembered as one of the first horror writers. People still love reading his chilling stories today.

Fiction Writers

Poe is said to have invented the modern detective story.

found that the noise was not within my ears.

... It was a low, dull, quick sound — much such a sound as a watch makes when enveloped in cotton. I gasped for breath — and yet the officers heard it not. I talked more quickly ... but the noise steadily increased. I arose and argued ... in a high key ... but the noise steadily increased.

The passage is told from the point of view of the main character, who is also a madman. Why does he hear the old man's heartbeat? Why does it get louder? What do you suppose the officers think of our narrator?

Let's Compare

Both passages are full of suspense. Each causes readers to nervously wonder what will happen next.

Author London uses words like "shock," "every moment," "peril," and "club and fang" to show that Buck faces immediate dangers. Readers are left excited to find out what will happen to Buck and

Much of the suspense in London's passage comes from its setting. Both the Alaskan wilderness and the characters located there are immediate dangers to Buck.

> A story's **climax** is its most exciting and interesting part.

what he will do to survive it all. There is an unknown adventure to come.

Though short, Poe's passage shows the story's **climax** of suspense. He repeats "noise" and "increase" to show that the heartbeat will not stop haunting the narrator. Words like "gasped" and "high key" also show the effect that the beating has on the madman. Readers must excitedly wonder if the madman's nervous behavior will give him away to the police.

The Call of the Wild *and "The Tell-Tale Heart" are both suspenseful stories. Readers of the stories have a sense of excitement as they wait to see what will happen next.*

Write Your Own Fiction

1. Think of a plot, or story, that you like. If a story entertains and interests you, it will likely be interesting to readers, too.

2. Define your characters and settings. Write down words to describe these elements with as much detail as possible.

Successful writers are also passionate readers. If you want to be a writer, you should read as much as you can.

3. What kinds of conflict will be in your story? Will the conflicts be between characters, between a character and a force, or within

a character? Make some detailed notes about the conflicts you see taking place in your story.

4. Choose a narrator for your story. What point of view will your narrator have?

5. Define your story themes. Is your story about survival, discovery, friendship, peace, or power? Write down your ideas.

6. Now start writing your story! Reread your notes whenever you need ideas. Remember that there is a story within you that you can write down.

Being a writer can be hard work. Stick with it! The more you write, the better your writing will be.

GLOSSARY

character A person in a story.

conflict A struggle that exists in a story that can be among characters, within a character, or between a character and something else.

first person A narration style in which a character tells the story and uses "I."

literary Related to or used in written works.

literary elements Parts that make up any novel or short story (for example: plot, character, theme, et cetera).

plot The series of events that form a story.

point of view The position or way in which the story is understood and related to readers.

setting Where a story takes place.

suspense A feeling of nervousness or excitement caused by wondering what will happen next

theme The subject of a work of literature or other art form.

third person A narration style in which a speaker outside of the story tells it using "he" or "she."

villain A character who does very bad things on purpose.

Books

Fandel, Jennifer. *You Can Write Awesome Stories.* North Mankato, MN: Capstone Press, 2012.

Ganeri, Anita. *I Can Write Narratives and Journals.* Chicago, IL: Heinemann Library, 2013.

Loewen, Nancy. *Once Upon a Time: Writing Your Own Fairy Tale.* Minneapolis, MN: Picture Window Books, 2009.

Lynette, Rachel. *Frank and Fiona Build a Fictional Story.* Chicago, IL: Norwood House Press, 2014.

Websites

Because of the changing nature of Internet links, Rosen Publishing has developed an online list of websites related to the subject of this book. This site is updated regularly. Please use this link to access the list:

http://www.rosenlinks.com/BCCL/Fict

INDEX

STATISTICS

STATISTICS

by Jane Jonas Srivastava

illustrated by John J. Reiss

Thomas Y. Crowell Company   New York

YOUNG MATH BOOKS

Edited by Dr. Max Beberman, Director of the Committee on
School Mathematics Projects, University of Illinois

BIGGER AND SMALLER
by Robert Froman

MATHEMATICAL GAMES FOR ONE OR TWO
by Mannis Charosh

CIRCLES
by Mindel and Harry Sitomer

ODDS AND EVENS
by Thomas C. O'Brien

COMPUTERS
by Jane Jonas Srivastava

PROBABILITY
by Charles F. Linn

THE ELLIPSE
by Mannis Charosh

RIGHT ANGLES: PAPER-FOLDING GEOMETRY
by Jo Phillips

ESTIMATION
by Charles F. Linn

RUBBER BANDS, BASEBALLS AND DOUGHNUTS:
A BOOK ABOUT TOPOLOGY
by Robert Froman

FRACTIONS ARE PARTS OF THINGS
by J. Richard Dennis

GRAPH GAMES
by Frédérique and Papy

STRAIGHT LINES, PARALLEL LINES,
PERPENDICULAR LINES
by Mannis Charosh

LINES, SEGMENTS, POLYGONS
by Mindel and Harry Sitomer

WEIGHING & BALANCING
by Jane Jonas Srivastava

LONG, SHORT, HIGH, LOW, THIN, WIDE
by James T. Fey

WHAT IS SYMMETRY?
by Mindel and Harry Sitomer

Edited by Dorothy Bloomfield, Mathematics Specialist,
Bank Street College of Education

LESS THAN NOTHING IS REALLY SOMETHING *by Robert Froman*

STATISTICS *by Jane Jonas Srivastava*

VENN DIAGRAMS *by Robert Froman*

Library of Congress Cataloging in Publication Data   Srivastava, Jane Jonas.   Statistics.   (A Young
Math Book) SUMMARY: A simple introduction to the concept and uses of statistics.   1. Statistics—
Juvenile literature.   [1. Statistics]   I. Reiss, John J., illus.   II. Title.   HA29.S73   001.4'22
72-7559   ISBN 0-690-77299-8   ISBN 0-690-77300-5 (lib. bdg.)

2   3   4   5   6   7   8   9   10

STATISTICS

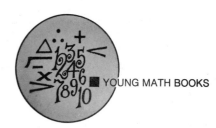

YOUNG MATH BOOKS

Count the number of trees on your street.

Count the number of people in your apartment.

Count the number of crayons in your desk at school.

Each of the numbers you counted can be used as a STATISTIC. Statistics are found by counting.

Statistics tell us many things:
    They tell how many people live in a
       country.
    They tell how many children ride a bus to
       school.
    They tell how many people like Bright
       White toothpaste.

Statistics are a way of measuring the world we live in.

Your school keeps a record of your address, your age, your height, and your weight. These are statistics about you.

Many countries take a CENSUS every ten years. The census is a count of the people who live in a country, and a count of other statistics about the country.

The government sends a letter or census taker to each house, asking questions such as:

How many people live here?
How old are the people who live here?
Do you own a car in this family?
Do you have a dog?

Census takers also ask questions of farmers and bankers, butchers, bakers, and candlestickmakers. What kind of questions do you think they ask these people?

You could take a census of your school. You might count the number of teachers, the number of classrooms, the number of doors. What else could you count in your census?

What do you think? Would the statistics for my school be the same as the statistics for your school?

People who use statistics are called STATISTICIANS. From a census, statisticians know how many people live in a country, and how many bushels of corn the farmers in that country have grown.

Sometimes statisticians take a POLL or a SURVEY to find out what kinds of things people like. A poll may be taken to find out how many children like baseball better than football, or to find out how many parents want a traffic light in front of the school.

It would take a long time for statisticians to ask <u>all</u> the parents whether they want a traffic light in front of the school.

Instead, they poll a SAMPLE: a few parents who can stand for all the rest.

Actually, the statistics from a sample tell you only about the sample. But they will probably be true for the whole group if the sample that was chosen was a fair sample, if it had the same share of each kind of person as the whole group. Useful statistics come from a sample that is a fair sample of everybody. They can be used for making a good guess about the whole group. The bigger the sample, the more chance that it is a fair one. Of course, the fairest sample of all is the sample which includes everybody.

Let's do an experiment to see what difference the size of the sample can make.

In a corner, all by yourself, count out a large number of red beads: 53, or 76, or 91, or 154.

Then count out **an equal** number or a different number of yellow beads. Write the number of red and yellow beads on a piece of paper so you won't forget how many of each you counted. Put the piece of paper in your pocket, and mix up the counted beads in a big paper bag.

If you do not have beads, you can use jelly beans, or blocks, or anything you like. Whatever you choose should be of the same shape and size but different colors.

Now ask a friend to take 5 beads out of the bag. Keep a record of the beads he pulls out.

BEADS TAKEN OUT
RED   YELLOW
 || |||

Ask him to guess whether there were more red beads, or more yellow beads, or the same number of red beads and yellow beads in the bag. Ask him whether he thinks there are any white beads in the bag. Ask him to write down his guess. Don't tell him whether his guess is right or wrong.

Now ask him to pull out some more beads until he has taken out 25 beads altogether. Ask him to guess again. Maybe his guess will be the same as before; maybe it will be different. Ask him to write down his new guess, but don't tell him yet whether his guess is right or wrong.

Your friend can continue taking out beads and keeping a record of their colors. He can make new guesses whenever he likes. Each time he guesses, he is using a larger sample of the beads. Are his guesses about the whole bag of beads more correct when the sample is big or small?

Do you know which fruit the children in your school like best? Instead of asking every child in the school, you can poll a sample. You might pick 5 children from each classroom. How will you pick your sample so it will be a fair sample? Will you choose 5 children from the front row, or 5 children who are wearing brown shoes, or the 5 children who finish their work first? Will it be fair if you pick only those children who like apples?

If there are 8 classrooms in your school, and you pick 5 children from each class, there will be 40 children in your sample. Suppose you find that:

16 children like apples
8 children like bananas
4 children like pears
8 children like oranges
4 children like blueberries.

You can show your statistics in a list called a TABLE:

Number of Children	Fruit Liked Best
16	apples
8	bananas
8	oranges
4	pears
4	blueberries

You can also show your statistics in pictures called GRAPHS.

Ask all the children who like the same kind of fruit to stand together in groups of four. Ask each group to name one child to tell which kind of fruit the group likes best.

Draw a picture of the 10 children who were chosen. Each child stands for four children. This picture is called a PICTOGRAPH.

You were lucky. There were no children left over from the groups of four. With a different sample, you might not be able to get even groups of four or three or five. Then it would be harder to draw a pictograph.

This is a BAR GRAPH.

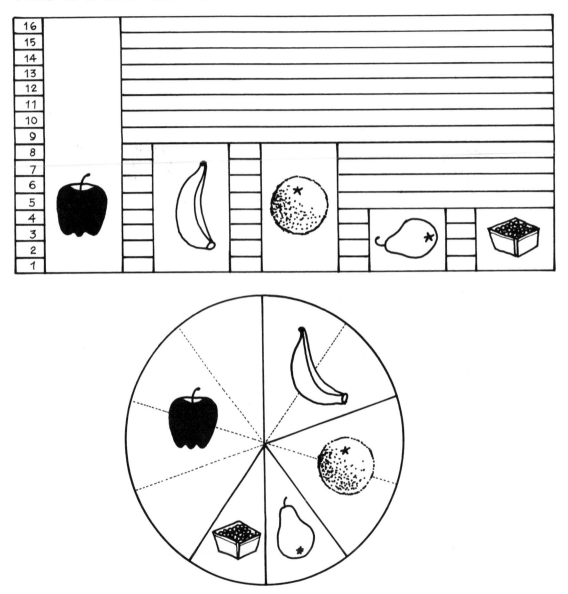

This is a CIRCLE GRAPH.

In your sample, 16 children liked apples best. The number of children who like apples best may change. You can show this change in a LINE GRAPH:

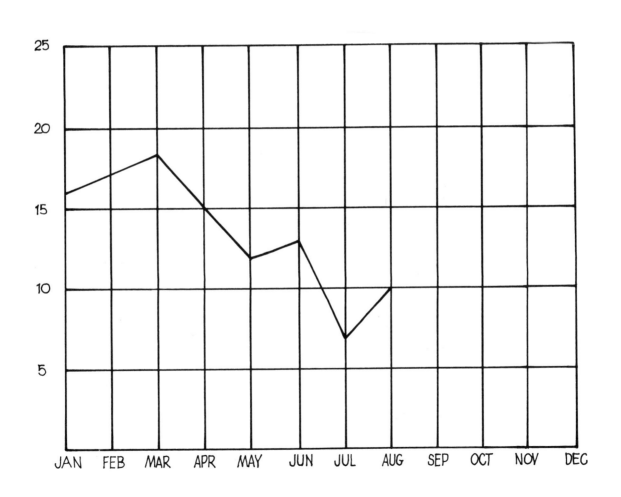

Take a poll of your classmates to find out how many want to have recess in the afternoon instead of in the morning. Take a poll of the people in your family to find out how many like spinach and how many like corn. Draw graphs to show these statistics.

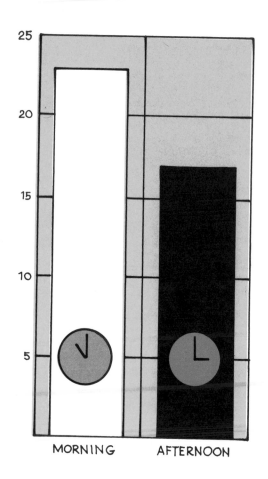

MORNING   AFTERNOON

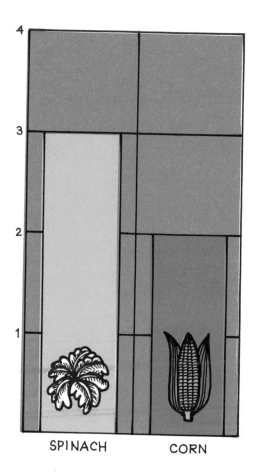

SPINACH   CORN

Statistics can be very useful. Farmers use them to decide how much corn to grow. Bakers use them to decide how much bread to bake. The man who runs the store near your school could use your statistics to decide how many apples and bananas to keep in the store for children to buy. The owner of the supermarket near your home could use your statistics to decide how much spinach and corn to keep in the store for people to buy.

Car makers use statistics which tell them how many cars were bought this year, last year, and the years before to see if the number is getting bigger or smaller. This helps them to decide how many cars they should make for next year. They use statistics about today and yesterday to make a better guess about tomorrow.

Statistics are also used to try to make people buy certain things. If an advertisement says that 1,463,251 people use Bright White toothpaste or that people who use Bright White toothpaste have fewer cavities, you are supposed to think that Bright White toothpaste is the best kind to buy.

In order to understand a statistic, it is important to know exactly what the statistic is all about.

On page 1 you counted the number of people in your apartment. Did you count your goldfish or your dog or your new baby sister as one of the people in your apartment? It is important to know exactly what has been counted.

Who did the counting? If your little brother, who is just learning to count, and sometimes makes mistakes, counted the trees on your street, would he get the same number as you did?

When was the counting done? Are there the same number of people in your apartment at night when every one is sleeping in their beds as there are in the day when some of the children are at school and some of the grown-ups are at work?

Where was the counting done? Did you count trees on a city street or on a town street? Would the number be different if you lived near a forest or near a desert?

Make a list of the statistics you read in the newspaper or hear on TV. Your list may look like this:

40,000 Supercars were sold last year.

Miniclock is the smallest clock on the market.

1 out of every 5 families owns a Zingmobile.

40% of the people in Bigtown use gas heat.

Everybody likes Superscoop ice cream cones.

Which of these statistics tell you how many were counted, who counted them, what was counted, where and when it was counted? Do any of them tell you whether a sample was used? Do they say how the sample was chosen? Was it a fair sample?

The word *statistic* is a tongue twister. Try saying it ten times fast. Statistics can be mind twisters, too. When you read a statistic, be careful that it does not twist your mind and make you believe something that is not true.

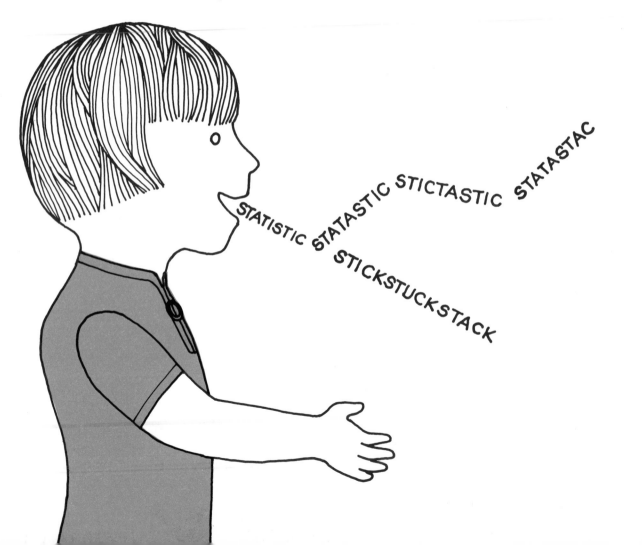

STATISTIC STATASTIC STICTASTIC STATASTAC

STICKSTUCKSTACK

Statistics showing how many cars were sold
20 years ago may not be very useful in deciding
how many cars to make next year.

SUPERCARS SOLD 20 YEARS AGO

25

The 1,463,251 people who use Bright White toothpaste may use it to draw pictures instead of to brush their teeth.

A friend who tells you that he counted only 7 children in his census of the school may have counted at recess time, when most children were playing outside.

Ask questions each time you read a statistic.
The answers to your questions will tell you
whether you can trust the statistic.

Now you know what statistics are, how to find them, and how to use them wisely.

Have fun collecting statistics about today's world.

Have fun using statistics to guess about tomorrow's world.

ABOUT THE AUTHOR

Jane Jonas Srivastava has been teaching mathematics since receiving her master's degree in education. She has worked in the University of Illinois Arithmetic Project in Watertown, Massachusetts, and in Simon Fraser University's project to initiate a new primary arithmetic program in local schools.

Mrs. Srivastava now teaches elementary school. Her husband is a professor of biological sciences at Simon Fraser University. They live in North Vancouver, British Columbia.

ABOUT THE ILLUSTRATOR

John J. Reiss was born and now lives in Milwaukee, Wisconsin. He studied with Josef Albers at Black Mountain College, and he has also studied with Robert Motherwell and Lyonel Feininger among other well-known artists.

Mr. Reiss won an AIGA award for *Numbers* which he both wrote and illustrated. He was chosen by the Children's Book Council in 1971 to design the Library Week mobile.

He collects modern drawings and prints. Mr. Reiss's wife is also an artist, and together they collect primitive art. For recreation Mr. Reiss likes to climb mountains. He has climbed in Canada and has traveled in Europe as well as in Latin America.